A Very Improbable Story

A Math Adventure

Edward Einhorn   *Illustrated by* **Adam Gustavson**

iʌi Charlesbridge

To my niece, Felicia Abigail: Just born, but I believe the probability you will be lovable, beautiful, and brilliant is very, very high—E. E.

For David and Ian—A. G.

Published by Charlesbridge
85 Main Street
Watertown, MA 02472
(617) 926-0329

Library of Congress Cataloging-in-Publication Data
Einhorn, Edward (Edward Arthur), 1970–
    A very improbable story / by Edward Einhorn ; illustrated by Adam Gustavson.
        p. cm.
    Summary: Waking up one morning and finding a talking cat on his head, Ethan is informed that the cat will not leave until he has won a game of probability.
    ISBN 978-1-57091-871-1 (reinforced for library use)
    ISBN 978-1-57091-872-8 (softcover)
[1. Cats—Fiction. 2. Mathematics—Fiction.] I. Gustavson, Adam, ill. II. Title.
PZ7.E34445Ve 2007
[E]—dc22   2006028095

Printed in China
(hc) 10 9 8 7 6 5 4 3 2 1
(sc) 10 9 8 7 6 5 4 3 2 1

Illustrations done in oil on Rives BFK printmaking paper
Display type and text type set in Knock Out and Galliard
Color separations by Chroma Graphics, Singapore
Printed and bound by Everbest Printing Company, Ltd.,
  through Four Colour Imports Ltd., Louisville, Kentucky
Production supervision by Brian G. Walker
Designed by Sarah McAbee

One morning Ethan woke up with a cat on his head. There was nothing improbable about that. Ethan's cat, Snowy, sometimes curled up there to sleep. But this was different. The cat on Ethan's head wasn't his cat!

4

"What in the—what are you doing up there?" Ethan tried to remove the animal. The cat wouldn't budge.

"I wouldn't do that," said the cat.

"You can talk?"

"Kid, you're a master of the obvious," said the cat.

6

"How is . . . what kind of . . . I can't believe this!" Ethan stammered as he scrambled out of bed.

"Well, I'm no ordinary cat." The creature stretched. "My name is Odds, and I like to play games of probability—how likely it is that something will happen."

"What does that have to do with being on my head?" Ethan looked in the mirror.

"Win a game and I'll get off," said Odds.

"I'd love to play a game," said Ethan, "but I have soccer in an hour. It's the last match of the season."

"Oh?" asked Odds. "Do you usually play soccer with a cat on your head?"

"Come on! The team's counting on me," Ethan pleaded. Odds didn't move.

Ethan shook his head back and forth. No good. He did jumping jacks, a cartwheel, and a handstand. Odds held on.

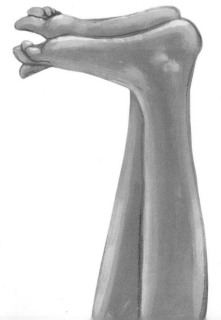

"Hey kid, I see an easy way out of this. That can of coins on your shelf is an opportunity."

"How?" asked Ethan.

"If you can pull out a dime without looking, I'll get off your head."

Ethan reached in and pulled out a penny.

"Ta-dah!" sang Odds. "You lose."

"Maybe a shower will convince you to leave," Ethan muttered. "Cats don't like to get wet, right?"

Ethan was right. Odds didn't like gettin[g] wet. He howled, but he didn't get off.

Ethan turned off the shower. "So, the on[ly] way you'll get off is if I win your game?"

"That's right," said Odds.

Ethan put on his shorts and his soccer jersey. The neck hole was just big enough for Odds to fit through.

"Don't put on your socks yet," ordered Odds. "It can be our next game. All of your pairs of socks are different. You'll win if you can pull out 2 matching socks without looking."

Ethan reached into the drawer and pulled out a striped sock. "So now all I have to do is pull out a matching one," he said.

"It's not as easy as it sounds," warned Odds. "With 10 pairs of socks, you have a very low probability of finding a match."

"Here goes nothing!" said Ethan. He took a deep breath and pulled out a sock.

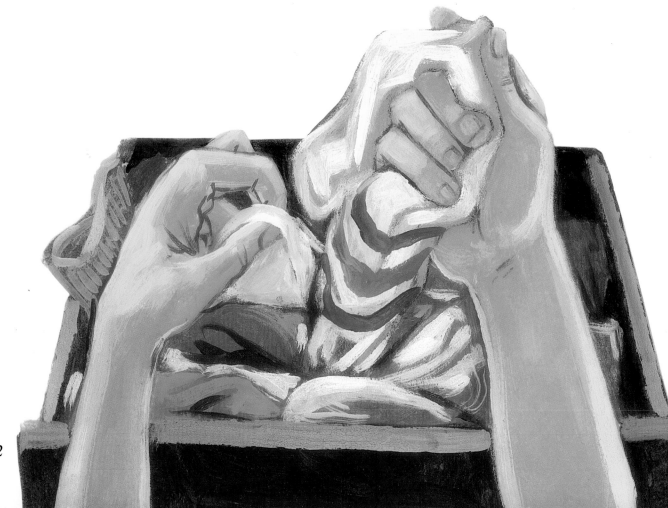

"Ta-dah!" sang Odds. "You lose. After you pulled out the first sock there were 19 single socks left. So there was only 1 sock out of 19 that would have let you win."

"Is that what they call bad odds?" asked Ethan.

"Some do," admitted Odds, "though I would never put the words 'bad' and 'odds' together."

"So the odds were 1 out of 19," said Ethan. "But now they're 1 out of 18." He pulled out another sock and groaned. This one had stars on it.

"I think it's time for a new game," Odds yawned.

At that moment the door flew open and Ethan's little sister Cindy ran in. "KITTY!" she squealed. "Hi, Ethan. Hello, kitty!"

"Hello," said Odds, squinting down at her.

"Let's play!" Cindy squealed, grabbing at Odds's tail.

Odds pulled his tail away. "I only play probability games," he sniffed.

"Wanna snack?" Cindy asked, picking up Ethan's bag of marbles.

"Cats don't eat mar—Marbles, that's it!" Ethan exclaimed, taking the bag from her. "That would make a great probability game, wouldn't it?"

"Maybe," Odds admitted.

Ethan dumped the marbles onto the rug and counted. "There are 25 white, 25 yellow, 25 green, and 25 blue—100 in all."

Cindy counted, too. "One, two, five kazillion."

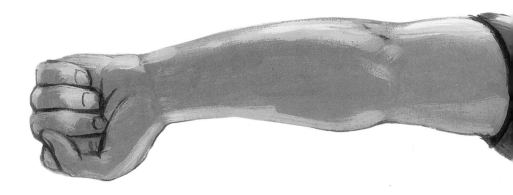

"Here's a probability game," said Ethan. "I'll pick out a white one. I have only a 25 in 100 chance of doing that."

"That's too easy," said Odds. "That's the same as odds of 1 in 4."

Cindy said, "I know a game. Let's jump on the marbles!" She waved her arms, ready to leap.

"No!" cried out Odds and Ethan together.

Ethan made Cindy sit on the bed.

"How about this?" said Ethan. "I'll try to pull out 2 white marbles. That would have a low probability."

Odds shrugged.

"What's pro-ba-ba-blib-idy?" asked Cindy. "Why are you doing that?"

"I'm trying to figure out my chance. That's what pro-ba-BIL-ity means." He arranged the marbles in groups of 2. "I'm putting together every combination of 2 colors to figure out how likely 2 white marbles would be.

"See, there are 16 combinations," he declared, "so the odds are 1 in 16!"

"Tough odds," purred the cat. "Let's play."

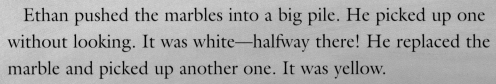

Ethan pushed the marbles into a big pile. He picked up one without looking. It was white—halfway there! He replaced the marble and picked up another one. It was yellow.

"Ta-dah!" sang Odds. "You lose."

"Let me see!" demanded Cindy. Ethan sighed and showed her the mismatched marbles.

Cindy reached in and took out 2 white marbles. "I win!" she shouted.

"You cheated," Ethan said. "It's not a probability game if you look."

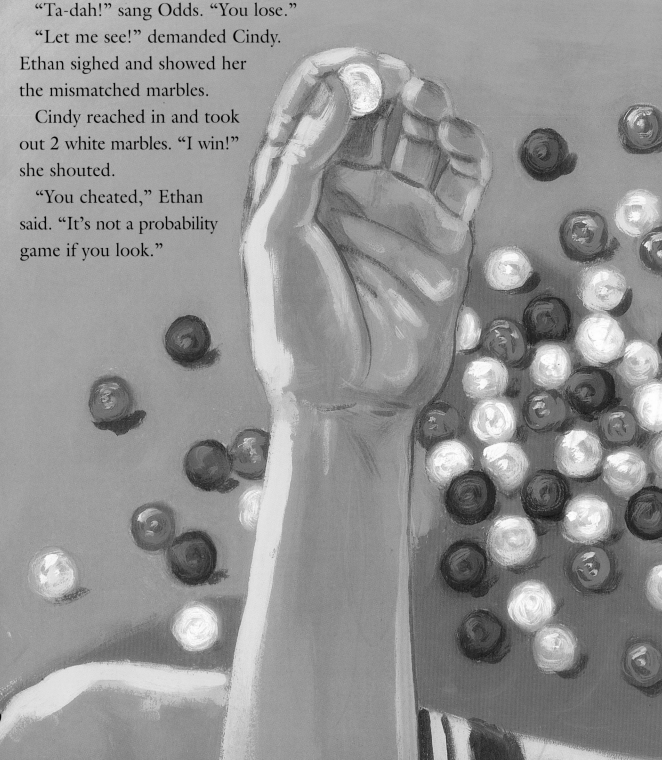

"Ethan! Cindy! Breakfast!"
their mom called.
"Bye, kitty," said Cindy.
She gave Odds a kiss and ran out
of the room.

21

"Please, Odds, I have to go to my soccer—" Ethan stopped.
"Hey, wait, maybe soccer can be a probability game. If we
score 5 goals, but make 25 attempts, then we have a, um,
1 in 5 chance, and . . ."

"And?" asked Odds.

Ethan sighed. "I don't know. I'll think about it during breakfast. I hope no one's in the kitchen," he said, putting on his cowboy hat to hide Odds.

Cindy had already finished her breakfast. The kitchen was empty.

"It's Oatie-Woofs!" said Ethan, scooping up a handful of dog-shaped cereal. "Try them. They're delicious."

Odds hissed. "Don't much care for dogs," he growled. "They're always trying to beat the odds."

"But look!" exclaimed Ethan. "There are five shapes: poodles, beagles, collies, Saint Bernards, and pugs. That could be a probability game."

"Show me," said Odds.

"It's like the marbles game, but now we have 5 different shapes." Ethan pushed them into pairs. "There are 25 possible pairs. Which one would you like me to try for?"

"Two pugs," said Odds. "They have the smallest teeth."

"Okay," said Ethan. He closed his eyes and mixed up the pieces. "I have a 1 in 25 chance." He picked up a piece of cereal. "A pug!" He replaced the piece and picked up another.

25

"This is it," he said, slowly opening his hand.

It was another pug. "Ta-dah! I won!" Ethan shouted, holding up the winning pair. "I did something with a low probability! This is great!"

He began jumping up and down but suddenly stopped. "I don't want to be a poor sport, but you did say you'd get off my head if I won . . ."

Odds landed with a *whomp* on the table. "Nice going, kid. Sure you don't want to keep playing? It might make you a better soccer player."

Ethan paused. "You know, it just might."

"Oh, really?" Odds purred. "Do tell."

"In the last game, I shot on goal 20 times and scored 5 of those times," Ethan explained. "My chance of getting a goal is 5 in 20, or 1 in 4. I should be able to make 1 goal every 4 tries."

"Good odds," admitted Odds.

"But look at this," Ethan said. He made a drawing to show how he made the shots.

"I tried to score with a low shot 15 times. Only 3 of those went in, so I have a 3 in 15 chance of scoring with a low shot. That's the same as a 1 in 5 chance.

"I tried 5 times to score with a high shot. Since 2 of those scored, I have a 2 in 5 chance of getting a goal with a high shot. A 2 in 5 chance is better than a 1 in 5 chance..

"Which means," Ethan concluded, "that I have great odds if I aim high."

"Not bad, kid," said Odds.

Ethan's mother called from the garage. "Ethan! It's time to go. You don't want to be late for the big match."

Odds jumped down from the table and walked toward the door. "It's time for me to hit the road, kid. With probability on your side, you're going to win that game, right?"

Ethan smiled as he opened the door. "Probably."

The History of Mathematical Probability

Two famous French mathematicians, Blaise Pascal and Pierre de Fermat, developed the theory of mathematical probability in 1654, following a dispute between gamblers over a dice game. In 1812 Pierre-Simon Laplace applied the theory to scientific and practical problems. Now probability is used in fields such as psychology, economics, and genetics, among many others.

Try it: Close your eyes and open this book to a page at random. What's the probability that a picture will be on the page?

Answer: Your odds are 32 in 32, or 1 in 1. You have a 100 percent chance!